Affirmations: 33 affirmations that will transform your life

How to manifest all that you want, wish and desire.

N.D. LONDON

Copyright & Disclaimer

This document is geared towards providing reliable information regarding the topic and issue covered. The publication is sold with the idea that the publisher is not required to render accounting, officially permitted or otherwise qualified services. If advice is necessary, legal or professional, a practiced individual in the profession should be appointed.

In no way is it legal to reproduce, duplicate, or transmit any part of this document in either electronic means or printed format. The recording of this publication is strictly prohibited. Any storage of this document is not allowed unless with written permission from the publisher.

The information provided herein is stated to be truthful and consistent. Any liability - in terms of inattention or otherwise - by any usage or abuse of any policies, processes, or directions contained within is the solitary and utter responsibility of the recipient reader. Under no circumstances will any legal responsibility or blame be held against the publisher for any reparation, damages, or monetary loss due to the information herein, either directly or indirectly.

Respective authors own all copyrights not held by the publisher.

The information herein is offered for informational purposes solely and is universal as so. The presentation of the information is without a contract or any type of guarantee assurance.

The trademarks that are used are without consent, and the trademark's publication is without permission or backing by the trademark owner. All trademarks and brands within this book are for clarifying purposes only and are owned by the owners themselves, not affiliated with this document.

All rights reserved.

Table of Contents

Introduction

The study of numerology shows that the number thirty-three is an incredibly powerful master number that symbolises enlightenment and guidance whilst encouraging blessings and inspiration into our lives.

I have chosen to provide you with thirty-three powerful affirmations as I believe that, by introducing these powerful words into your daily routine while using the number thirty-three as a guiding force, you will encourage your cells in your mind and your body to heal and manifest what you want, dream of, and desire into your life.

Many of us tend to underestimate the power of our thoughts, disregarding them as meaningless and lifeless, believing that our thoughts cannot influence reality in any way when, in actual fact, our thoughts are the opposite of that. Our thoughts create a chain reaction to everything that goes on in our orbit and they are, in fact, meaningful, influencing absolutely everything that becomes our reality.

If you pay attention and watch your thoughts throughout the day, you will be amazed at how these thoughts affect your emotions, state of mind, body language, and overall behaviour. When you think positive thoughts, they attract positive things into your life, and this is because positive thoughts cause a shift in your focus on events and experiences.

It is natural for us to want to live a happy, fulfilled, and successful life, and one of the ways that we can achieve this dream is to dedicate some time every day to recite as many positive affirmations as possible.

By introducing positive words and thoughts into your heart and mind with affirmations, you initiate a chain reaction that makes it a habit for positive thoughts to come in, one after the other. In other words, a positive thought process creates a potential for infinite positive outcomes.

Feeding your mind positive thoughts at all times will train your brain to start believing what it hears. The effects will begin to flow through your words and actions, welcoming in positive energies that gravitate into your life, relationships, work, finances, and health.

What's the link between affirmations and the Law of Attraction?
Affirmations and the Law of Attraction work intricately together. Both of these energies entwine together in making our words, thoughts, and feelings our reality.

The Law of Attraction works subconsciously and consciously with our bodily vibrations and energy fields as a magnet, drawing things, thoughts, and feelings towards us based on what we have been thinking and saying.

With every word that we think and utter, we are communicating with the universe and, in turn, attracting back what we put out there.

Unfortunately, we have no idea how much potential lies deep within us. Because of this ignorance, we fail to check our thoughts and emotions so that they are aligned with what we want to manifest into our lives. When our thoughts and emotions are unaligned, the chances are we attract unwanted events into our lives.

Knowing that the Law of Attraction is at work in our lives is a great cause for celebration. Once you understand the power of this law, nothing will ever be the same again, as you will freely and effectively apply it in every area of your life. This will ultimately help you to create the future that you desire. You must be willing to work to seize every opportunity that comes your way in order reach your fullest potential.

This book will encourage your mind to break old habits and to focus on the goal at hand. Even if you're not a believer right now, the Law of Attraction is real. By introducing a routine of saying these powerful affirmations to yourself, you will be encouraging your body to welcome nothing but positivity into your life.

You are the artist of your life; your life is a blank canvas full of possibilities. With every thought that you have, you are creating mental images of your intended life, making choices and acting on them to release your innermost desires; as the artist, you are in control of your finished product, your reality. It is your responsibility to assess the mental pictures that you are creating in your mind. If you do not like them, ask yourself what you would like your finished picture to look like and then alter your thoughts to change them.

When it comes to the Law of Attraction, there is no catch! Irrespective of what you would like to have, be, or achieve in this life, holding on to the idea and creating a mental picture of it, seeing it in your mind's eye, will help you to manifest it into reality. It will not, however, just fall into your lap; once you have altered your mind-set, you will then have to work at accomplishing what has been spoken!

While there is infinite power in spoken words, the truth is that the real power lies deep inside you, in your thoughts and actions. It takes these things to reach your goals and dreams. In addition to saying these words, you must be willing to make a conscious effort to manage your time and skills wisely in order to allow what you desire to flow freely into your life. Now you know that you have the power to manifest all that you desire, there is nothing stopping you!

Chapter 1 - What are affirmations?

Affirmations refer to short, positive sentences aimed at influencing both the conscious and subconscious mind. They are the very powerful phrases that when you recite, think, or even hear them, they become your thoughts that, in turn, create your reality.

Every day, you have at least 45,000 to 51,000 thoughts that cross your mind. This translates to 150-300 thoughts every minute. Unfortunately, 80% of these thoughts are negative for most people.

But it does not have to be that way. The good news is that you can reverse that negativity by using positive affirmations. When you use affirmations, you alter your mind's thought process as well as influencing your actions, habits, and surroundings.

In other words, affirmations have the power to automatically change your mental image to an image that can be inspiring, energising, and motivating. It is through affirmations that the resulting mental images engrave in your subconscious mind, causing a change in habits, actions, and reactions based on the words that you affirm.

Affirmations play a significant role in creating positive and long-lasting changes in your life, they describe how and what you would like to be or attract into your life.

When you speak them, they motivate you and help you to focus on the goals that you would like to achieve. They alter the way that you think and behave. Each time you recite, read, or think of them, you feel positive, active, and energetic. When you are in that mind-set, you are in a better position to transform your internal and external worlds.

If you focus on positive affirmations long enough, you will not only produce but increase your desired outcomes. They can be used as method of self-improvement, can help to boost your self-confidence, lower negativity, improve your sense of self-worth, and positively affect your life.

For instance;

❖ In relation to your health, you can say things like "my mind and body are healthy and vibrant. I am energised and look forward to achieving all of my daily goals".
❖ If you need healing, you can say things like, "Today, healing, relaxation, and restoration are my priority".
❖ If you are looking for happiness and satisfaction in your life, you can use affirmations like, "I know I am not and do not have to be perfect for me to be happy. I am worthy of happiness; happiness is within me and is all around me".

If you use affirmations correctly and consistently, they will drive change and permanently influence your way of thinking. In other words, you will be in a better position to manage your expectations for positive outcomes and experience the desired outcome.

While there is power in the words that we speak, ultimately, it takes putting your thoughts into actions that will help you to reach your goals. In addition to saying these words, you must be willing to make a conscious effort to manage your time and skills wisely. If your affirmations are to be a kinder, more compassionate person, you will need to consciously take action after repeating these affirmations to act in the desired way. It will not just happen without you actively trying to do all that you can to create the desired results.

Learning and practicing affirmations will contribute to rewiring your mind so that you can reverse the effects of negative beliefs and habits, and replace them with a set of positive, self-nurturing ones. Your goals become clearer and achievable because your sense of self-belief grows stronger.

When you start to craft your own statements, ensure that you use words that resonate with you at an emotional, physical, and spiritual level, and that they are centred around the things that you want and not what you do not want. If you are unclear on what you want , take some time to meditate to see if your wants, wishes, and desires become clearer to you.

Write them down, record them, sing them, or silently repeat them; whatever method you choose to use in your routine is fine, as long as it resonates with you and feels good for you, that's all that matters.

Remember that your affirmations have the power to yield incredible outcomes. Initially, they may feel uncomfortable, strange, unbelievable, or even ineffective at first. However, you must be willing to overcome these initial thoughts and persevere in order to train your mind that this is your reality.

Being mindful of what affirmations you apply into your life can help you to eliminate the effect of negative thinking. You can use it as a powerful tool for rebuilding your strengths, healing your weaknesses, and creating the optimal future that you desire.

Chapter 2 - Types of affirmations

Acceptance Affirmations

"Accept – then act. Whatever the present moment contains, accept it as if you had chosen it. Always work with it, not against it. Make it, your friend and ally, not your enemy. This will miraculously transform your whole life." – Eckhart Tolle

Many people struggle with self-acceptance in every sense of the word. They think that acceptance is settling, admitting defeat, or failing. You may think that when you resist accepting things as they are, you will never be able to create what you truly desire. The truth is that this thought process is completely misguided. If you think this way, you are moving even further from the things that you truly desire.

Acceptance is not about settling or failure. Instead, it is acknowledging the things that you cannot change and allowing yourself to live in the present. It is an awakening to what is.

When you consciously accept things as they are, you choose to consciously create a robust foundation to move forward in the right direction to achieve your dreams. It is surrendering and relaxing into the trust of possibilities out there.

The best way to cultivate your acceptance is through the use of affirmations – hence, acceptance affirmations. When you use acceptance affirmations, you choose to open your mind to infinite possibilities the world has to offer. Everything will begin to unfold precisely as it should, because you trust the timing of your life. It is about knowing that things will be okay eventually, and what is meant for you will find its way into your arms.

Some of my favourite acceptance affirmations include;

- ❖ I choose to accept the things beyond my control so that I can move forward with the things that are within my control.
- ❖ I accept myself as I am – flaws, imperfections, and past mistakes – and choose to focus on learning from them so that I can grow.
- ❖ I accept happiness, love, joy, and fulfilment to see abundance in every area of my life.
- ❖ I choose to accept what is, without resisting.
- ❖ I accept responsibility for my actions because only I have the power to my happiness.
- ❖ I choose to accept others just the way they are without trying to change them and make them what they aren't.
- ❖ I accept my past and willingly release it so that I can move forward with my life.
- ❖ I accept my past mistakes and am grateful for them because they have shaped me into who I am today.

Action-Oriented Affirmations

"Dreams don't work unless you take action. The surest way to make your dreams come true is to live them." – Roy T. Bennett.

If you do not believe in something, there is no way you are going to act on it, which will inevitably mean that you will not create change.

You must first talk your mind into believing that your dream is possible and then act to achieve even the slightest outcome by reinforcing that possibility. Having a goal and acting on it will give you the power to alter what is possible for you.

Every one of us have big goals of what we would like to achieve; some bigger than others. You may also have ideas on how you intend to achieve those goals called milestones. These are necessary to get the ball rolling to achieve what you desire.

Regardless of other people's opinions and feedback, always remember to not let other people affect how and if you persevere. Do not give up on your goals and dreams because someone thinks they are silly, small, or irrelevant. Positive action-oriented affirmations will help you close this gap, turn around your beliefs, and take meaningful actions to achieve them. Action is the first step to seeing the change that you want.

Action-oriented affirmations are simply magical! The things that seemed impossible or unreasonable become reasonable and completely possible. After days, weeks, or months of using them, you start seeing magic happen. Suddenly, that idea you thought was crazy is brilliant. Whatever you wish to accomplish, remind yourself that repeating action-oriented affirmations each day will help you to trick your subconscious mind into working for you and solving that problem you thought was insurmountable.

Here are some action-oriented affirmations I use every day;

- ❖ I know that I can achieve my goals and reach my fullest potential.
- ❖ I am learning to trust myself and my abilities to achieve my goals.
- ❖ I am fully committed to turning my dreams and goals into my reality.
- ❖ I have what it takes to be all that I dream of becoming.
- ❖ I will get up every day and work towards achieving my set goals to ensure that I get what I desire.
- ❖ I know that if I act, anything is possible; even what seemed impossible at first can become my reality.
- ❖ I have the skills and abilities to achieve everything that I have set out to do today.
- ❖ I see consistent outcomes of my actions.
- ❖ What I do every day is bringing me closer and closer to achieving my goals.
- ❖ I can accomplish everything that I put my mind and heart to achieve.
- ❖ I can do it; I know I will.

Letting Go Affirmations

"The only thing a person can ever really do is keep moving forward. Take that big leap forward without hesitation, without once looking back. Simply forget the past and forge toward the future." – Alyson Noel

The most challenging thing for most people is having the ability to let go. As human beings, we hold on to people or things just so that we can feel important, loved, or less frightened. Perhaps you are holding on to the illusion of being in control when you are not. Or maybe you are holding on to past hurts or mistakes.

You must note that you cannot move forward with your life if you keep holding on to these things. To effect the change that you want, you must be willing to let go of all that is holding you back.

The best way to move past your hurt, mistakes, and delusions is to start crafting and repeating let go affirmations. Search deep within your life to find out what is standing in your way of happiness and fulfilment. Is it a past hurtful relationship or situation? Is it a past mistake or failure? Whatever it is, you can use affirmations to shift your focus and vision on to a path of personal empowerment, freedom, and happiness. Letting go of all that is holding you back from your dream life will go a long way in freeing your inner being.

Here are some of the affirmations that you can use to let go of all that;

- ❖ Fear will only keep me paralyzed and stuck in the past, and I will not let it.
- ❖ I relinquish control over things that I cannot change and choose to surrender completely to whatever life has in store for me.
- ❖ I choose to let go of everything and just go with the flow, taking the best from every moment.
- ❖ I choose to accept everything as is and will not try to change it.
- ❖ I choose to let go of everything that has happened in my past so that I can seize new opportunities in front of me and not be held back.
- ❖ My past has no power over my future.
- ❖ I let go of everything and anything that does not serve my purpose.
- ❖ Material belongings will not keep me from being happy and fulfilled.
- ❖ I choose to release all my fear-related feelings, thoughts, and sensations to keep moving into the future of my dreams.

Intention Affirmations

Intentions accompany all of your thoughts and actions. Interestingly, we do not think about these intentions in much depth, yet they often lead to frustrations. They are the reason we are in poor relationships, unsatisfying jobs, or even confused about our life's purpose.

Today, if you choose to focus on your intentions and spend your time setting them correctly, you will increase the chance of achieving your goals. The best way to do this is by using intention affirmations.

An intention affirmation is simply a statement that you can write down to express your intentions. Whenever you write something down, it forces you to reflect on it and how you plan on expressing it in reality. In other words, your intention affirmations will help you to explore what you mean and increase your accountability. You will gain a deeper understanding of yourself and reinforce your beliefs to your fullest potential.

A good intention affirmation has to be concise, clear, and inspiring. They must refer to a new way of living your life instead of just achieving goals. They must affirm what you want as though it is already happening, focusing on feeling, and expressing gratitude.

Examples of intention affirmations include;

- ❖ I want myself and my family to radiate health in mind and body.
- ❖ I support myself in choosing foods that make me feel and look my best.
- ❖ I am healing and renewing my body, soul, and mind by the power of healthy nutrition.
- ❖ I choose to make inner peace and remaining calm my top priorities.
- ❖ I choose to focus on positive self-talk and everything that steers me towards solutions, not problems.
- ❖ I choose to use highly effective wealth creation strategies to help me to achieve success and happiness in every area of my life.
- ❖ I am creating strategies to steer my family and myself to financial success and a healthy wellbeing.
- ❖ I love expressing myself in a way that allows my creative juices to flow.

Incorporating Affirmations

At times, you will realise that reaching your set goals and effecting the changes you want is more difficult than you thought. However, when you incorporate affirmations in your daily life, it becomes part of your daily strategy and plays a big part in your success.

What you need to note is that positive affirmations are not standalone solutions to your problems. Saying positive words can only get you so far.

Think about it. If you want to be more productive with your time and skills, you may use positive affirmations like, "I am productive and choose to use my time and skills wisely". However, if you say these words without incorporating them into your to-do list, they are just "words".

While there is power in spoken words, the truth is that real power lies deep inside you – your thoughts and actions. It takes these things to reach your goals. In addition to saying these words, you must be willing to make conscious efforts to manage your time and skills wisely.

To achieve your goals, you must act to effect change. Remind yourself that you can and will make changes by incorporating affirmations into your daily schedule.

The best ways to do this is;

- ❖ Write your affirmations in apps and send them to yourself as reminders.
- ❖ Journal your affirmations every morning, during the day, and before going to sleep.
- ❖ Record your affirmations in the third person and listen to them whenever you feel you are in self-doubt or need evidence of their truth.
- ❖ Create song playlists that support the message of your affirmations.
- ❖ Associate your affirmations with textures, textiles, or smells.
- ❖ Create a sketch of how you envision your affirmations.
- ❖ Turn your affirmations into chants or songs in familiar tunes that you can identify with and use when jogging, doing yoga, or going about your chores.
- ❖ Incorporate aromatherapy into your routine to help you remain mindful of your affirmations and goals.
- ❖ Take photos of things that inspire and motivate you to move forward with your life.

Gratitude Affirmations

"There is a calmness to a life lived in gratitude, a quiet joy."
– Ralph H. Blum

Most people do not realise that life does not respond to their wants, but what they choose to focus on. However, it is not easy to show gratitude when things are not going as planned or expected. When you choose to express gratitude, even when things are not going right, you enter into a new state of mind. You are not forcing or trying to rush things. You choose to take one day at a time by focusing on the things you desire to see.

In other words, the things that you focus on expand. When you express honest appreciation for what you have, it sends a signal to the universe that it is your priority. That way, it starts manifesting itself into your life more.

Being grateful for everything that you have, or are going through, does not mean you are living in denial of your current reality. It is choosing to work with it to create your desired reality.

Your future is listening.

Some of the gratitude affirmations you can use are;

- ❖ I am grateful for everything I have, and I am excited about what the future holds for me.
- ❖ I am grateful for the love I can give and the love that I receive.
- ❖ It doesn't matter what I have been through or what I am going through now because I know I can be grateful again.
- ❖ I am grateful for the help that the universe brings me even when its disguised or when I least expect it.
- ❖ I choose to be grateful now and welcome continuous blessings into my life.
- ❖ Every devastation that I have experienced has been an opportunity for transformation and my gratitude has evolved because of it.

Chapter 3 - Incorporating affirmations into your daily routine

"All that we are is the result of what we have thought. The mind is everything. What we think we become."
– Buddha

Affirmations should not be viewed as words that you say before moving on to the rest of your activities; you need to incorporate them into your life. Incorporating them into your daily routine should be meaningful, and the best way to achieve this is to choose affirmations that resonate with you. In other words, the affirmations that you choose to use should revolve around your needs. They should be a direct response to your negative self-talk, thoughts, and what you desire.

It is not about adopting positive affirmations that others use or about using the generic affirmations that you think you "should" be using. While this is not a bad place to start, creating your real change comes from using affirmations centred around things that you want or need to work on in your life.

If you wish to build your self-confidence and find yourself thinking, "I am worthless, I am inadequate, I cannot do this", you must create positive affirmations that directly counter these negative thoughts and self-talk. You can create positive affirmations like, "I am capable, I can do this, I have all that it takes to be the best, I am worthy, I am enough".

In order to counter negative thoughts, you should approach them by using a positive affirmation as a response. Each time a negative thought comes to mind, be prepared to automatically counter the thought with a positive response, with an "I am capable" type of affirmation.

The other way to incorporate them into your life is to pair those positive affirmations with part of your daily routine. Let's face; it is really difficult to find time to just sit and start using positive affirmations or even remember to do them at all. This is why pairing your affirmation time with things or activities that you already do will go a long way in helping you to develop new habits.

Pairing them with your routine allows you to say them while taking a shower, shaving, driving, exercising, or dressing. In the afternoon, you can also repeat them as you prepare lunch or wait to be served. As you drive home in the evening, while brushing your teeth, meditating, or journaling, you can repeat positive affirmations.

The most important thing is that you identify a solution that works perfectly well for you. Simply choose an activity every day and remind yourself that it is time for positive affirmations.

The third way to incorporate it into your life is to go beyond repetition. You must be willing to expand your learning by supplementing your affirmations with other tools.

For instance, if you want to build self-confidence, you can read books about your affirmation topic. It can be confidence, productivity, body image, and many others. You could also supplement it with Ted talks, podcasts, documentaries, and other contents available around the subject of your affirmation.

Additionally, you can keep a journal to help you stay on track with things that you have learned and where you can jot down general thoughts about your affirmations. Often, this is useful in noticing the progress that you are making and the changes that your affirmations are creating in your life.

Finally, get physical; when you experience a negative emotion, your body can react to it physically. You may feel like you have butterflies in the stomach, your heart may race faster, or you may feel tension in your neck. In the same way, when practicing your affirmations, you must note all the body sensations that it creates. Before you repeat your affirmations, take a step back, become mindful, and take a deep breath. Stand in front of a mirror and look yourself in the eye as you say them.

If possible, anchor your affirmations by placing your hands on the area of your physical body where you may be feeling discomfort from the negative emotion that you are feeling. For instance, if you feel sick to your stomach whenever you think of the upcoming seminar presentation, place your hand on it, and repeat your affirmations. This will help you feel more confident as you allow that affirmation to sink in.

Once you feel in touch with the physical response to emotional feelings that you have, you will have the ability to use them as cues to incorporate them into your routine throughout the day. If you feel some tightness in your shoulders or tension in your muscles, saying your affirmation as you touch these parts will combat both the emotional and physical discomforts.

Chapter 4 - Mastering your affirmations

You must remind yourself that when you change your thought process, everything else in your life changes. When you choose to use positive affirmations, you are consciously choosing to think positive thoughts that will create the kind of outcome that you desire in your future. In other words, they create a focal point that allows you to change your thinking.

According to research, the power of positive affirmations on the brain is quite simple. By affirming what you want and desire, you are subconsciously rewiring the brain and boosting psychological changes that, in turn, change your life.

The key to mastering the fruits of positive affirmations is to continually bombard the subconscious mind with positive affirmations so that it does not have time for negativity.

The point is for you to keep creating reality out of your imagination. In other words, repeat your affirmations until you have mastered them by heart. Repetition is everything in your journey to your dream life. If you choose to speak them aloud as your first mantra, your affirmations must have the following traits;

Firstly, ensure that they are in the present tense. The best way to do that is to declare your desires as though they are already true.

Secondly, they must be positive. In other words, ensure that your focus is on what you want and not what you don't want.

Thirdly, they should be short and clear. Bear in mind that brevity is in the soul of the wit. Making your affirmations short, simple, and clear makes it easier for you to not only say them, but also remember and act on them accordingly.

Fourthly, ensure that the element of action manifests itself in your affirmations so that they are impactful. The best way is to make them action-oriented. Visualise yourself in a situation where you take the lead and act. Tell yourself how determined you are to make it work again and then go ahead. This way, you are inducing the Law of Attraction in your life. Finally, attach emotions to your goals by using full-of-feeling words. In most cases, you will notice that people feel more energetic whenever they are emotional and passionate. Harnessing those emotions and passions will help you to create the outcome that you desire the most.

That said, what you must remember is that mental preparation will help you accept your affirmations and work on implementing them. Realise that a lack of belief in your affirmations as you speak them renders them useless.

Just like Shakespeare said, everything will be ready for you if your mind is ready too. Therefore, prepare your mind to have faith in what you want to manifest into your life. Don't throw away the power of your inner voice. Instead, use it to equip your mind to become aware of your thoughts. When you are tempted to get into self-doubt, tell yourself, "I am ready". This will help you steer your thoughts in the right direction.

Why affirmations should always be positive

Before we look at why affirmations should always be positive, we start with the effects of negative thoughts and words.

Think about it – when you are anxious or depressed, your worldview and perception of yourself are altered. These conditions tend to encourage us to have a negative mind-set.

Imagine watching the news – when you see positive and negative news, your mind tends to focus most on negative media and completely overlooks the positive ones. In other words, the mind tends to make negativity a comfort blanket that is not healthy.

That is why you need positive affirmations in your life to help you to change the negative thought processes that your mind tends to naturally cling to. This way, you can build a positive mind-set little by little until you completely change your outlook of the world and yourself.

Remember, what you repeatedly think and say about yourself is what you eventually become. Using positive affirmations in your life will help you to program your subconscious into building new habits, motivating you to go after your goals, and attract success.

The good thing about the human mind is that it can think and create what does not already exist. It can picture situations that are not in the current reality and cause them to manifest themselves in reality. Repeating positive affirmations allows your thoughts to sink into your subconscious mind and become part of who you are – the things that define you – attitudes, mind-set, and lifestyle. You will be able to carry these thoughts with you wherever you go, and that will make you grow stronger and affect and attract change in different areas of your life.

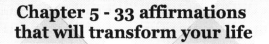

Chapter 5 - 33 affirmations that will transform your life

Every cell in my body is healthy.

Each cell is working intricately and exactly as it should be, weaving the web of wonder in my body, allowing me to radiate true health and happiness, and for that, I am thankful.

I manifest perfect health by making smart choices.

I let go of all bad habits and release all diseases from my body. I open my arms to health, happiness, and love in my life. Every cell in my body is vibrating with energy and functioning in perfect health.

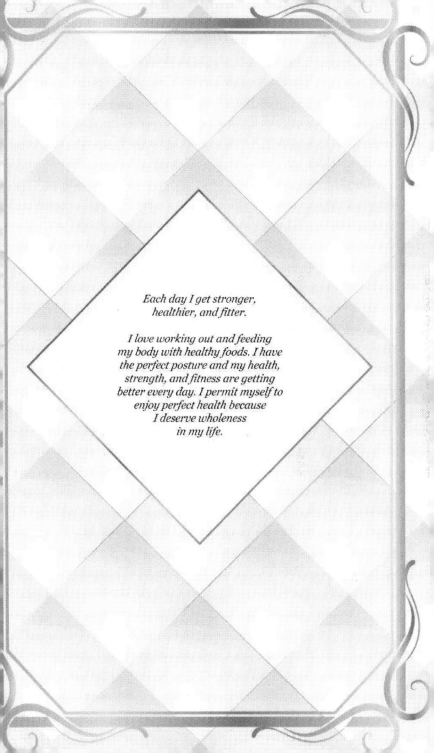

*Each day I get stronger,
healthier, and fitter.*

*I love working out and feeding
my body with healthy foods. I have
the perfect posture and my health,
strength, and fitness are getting
better every day. I permit myself to
enjoy perfect health because
I deserve wholeness
in my life.*

I am grateful to be alive.
I am thankful for the air that I breathe and
the life that I lead.

I am grateful that I have been given the
opportunity to wake up to another day.
I am grateful for all the blessings that I have.
It is my joy and pleasure to live each day
regardless of my circumstances.

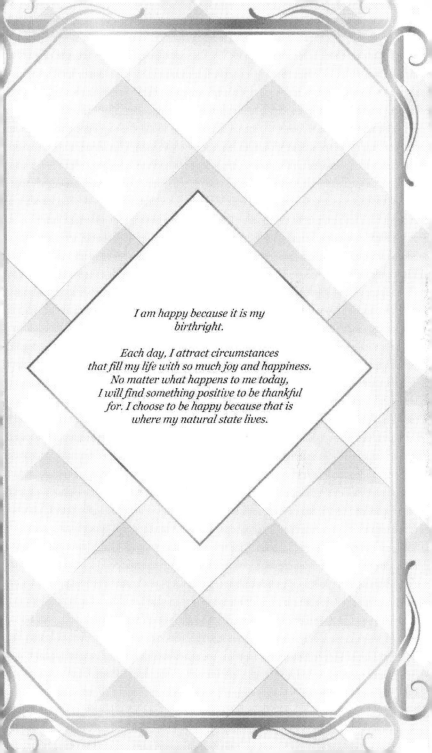

I am happy because it is my birthright.

Each day, I attract circumstances that fill my life with so much joy and happiness. No matter what happens to me today, I will find something positive to be thankful for. I choose to be happy because that is where my natural state lives.

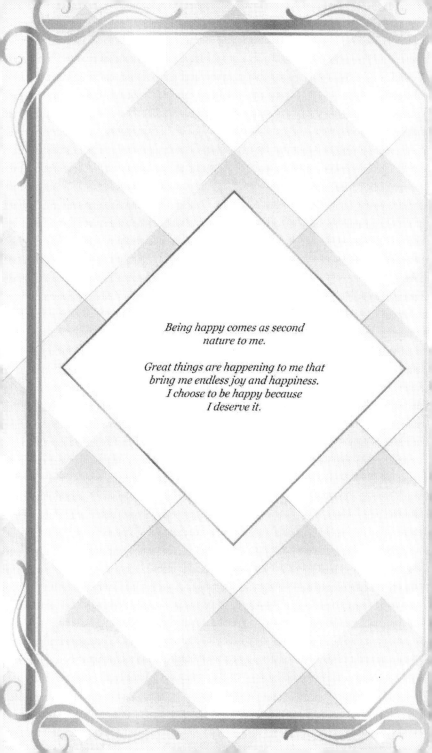

*Being happy comes as second
nature to me.*

*Great things are happening to me that
bring me endless joy and happiness.
I choose to be happy because
I deserve it.*

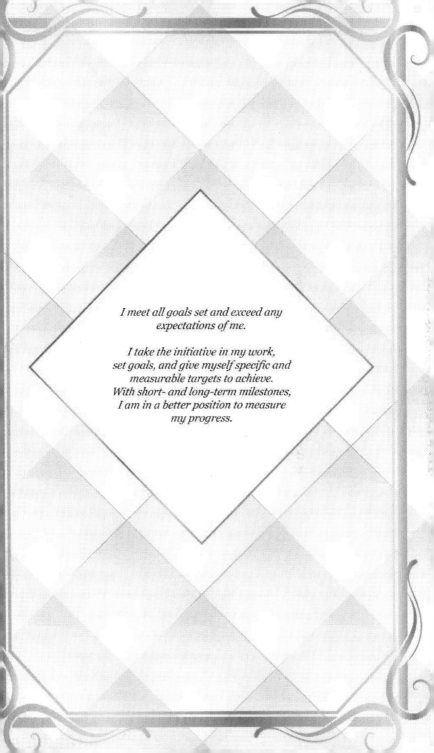

*I meet all goals set and exceed any
expectations of me.*

*I take the initiative in my work,
set goals, and give myself specific and
measurable targets to achieve.
With short- and long-term milestones,
I am in a better position to measure
my progress.*

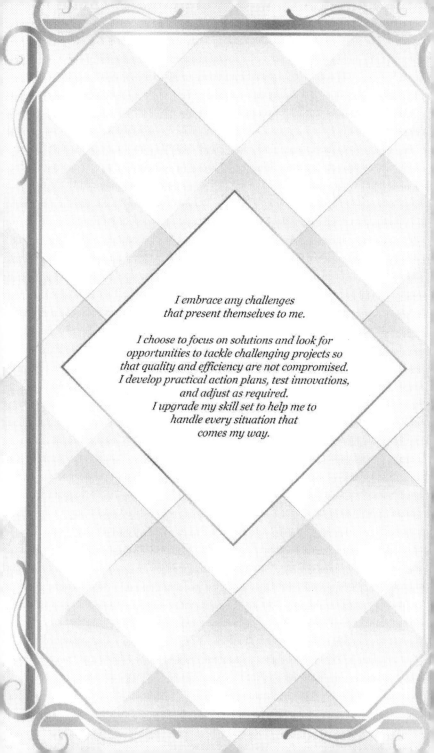

*I embrace any challenges
that present themselves to me.*

*I choose to focus on solutions and look for
opportunities to tackle challenging projects so
that quality and efficiency are not compromised.
I develop practical action plans, test innovations,
and adjust as required.
I upgrade my skill set to help me to
handle every situation that
comes my way.*

*My possibilities are endless, and
I am worthy of my dreams.*

*I choose to focus on my inner strengths
because that will bring me closer to realising
my goals. Having confidence in my abilities
and seizing every opportunity that comes
my way brings out hidden abilities.
Just seeing others move away from
their comfort zone inspires me to embrace
all of the possibilities that the universe
has in store for me.*

*Success and rewards come to me
easily and effortlessly because I excel
in all that I do.*

*I expect a positive outcome in all that
I do and, in turn, naturally attract them to me.
I am proud of my innate abilities to make
worthy contributions to my work and society,
and this allows for more success and
abundance in my life. I choose to set
incredibly high standards for myself
and live up to them.*

My actions create prosperity
and constantly attract opportunities that
will bring an abundance of wealth.

The Universe is always guiding and
supporting me to accomplish all of my goals
and desires. The wealth of the Universe is
always circulating in my life and bringing
me an avalanche of success and prosperity.
I choose to be driven, motivated,
and ambitious to bring more
success to my life.

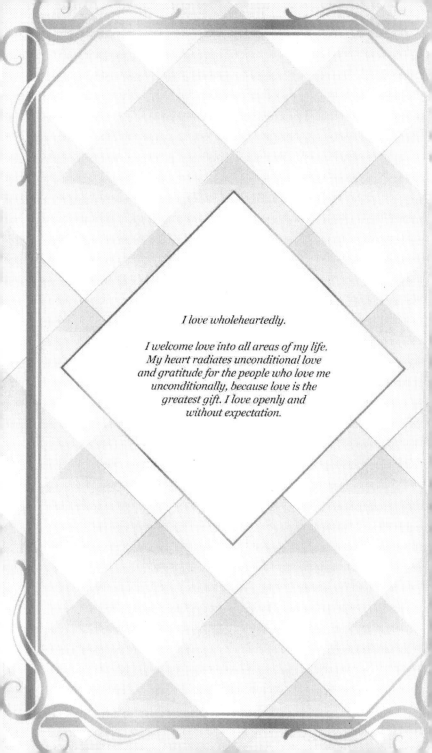

I love wholeheartedly.

*I welcome love into all areas of my life.
My heart radiates unconditional love
and gratitude for the people who love me
unconditionally, because love is the
greatest gift. I love openly and
without expectation.*

*If single and wanting
a partner:*

*The perfect person for me is coming
into my life sooner than I expect. I attract
healthy and strong relationships in my life.*

If married:

*My marriage will become stronger
and more stable every day because I choose
to honour my feelings and foster open
communication with my spouse.
Love flows freely and
abundantly to me.*

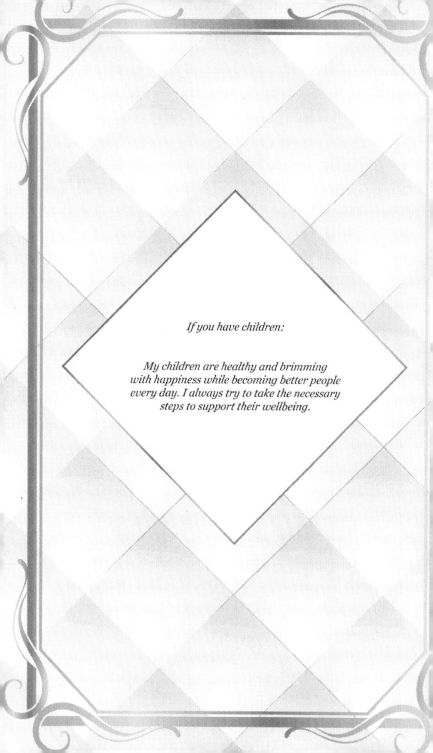

If you have children:

My children are healthy and brimming with happiness while becoming better people every day. I always try to take the necessary steps to support their wellbeing.

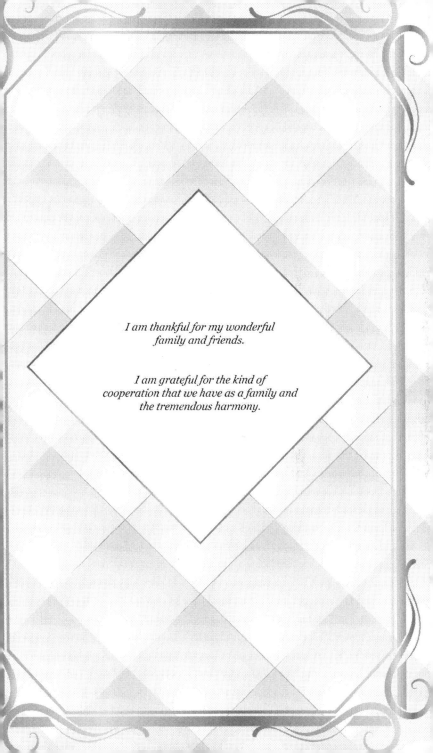

*I am thankful for my wonderful
family and friends.*

*I am grateful for the kind of
cooperation that we have as a family and
the tremendous harmony.*

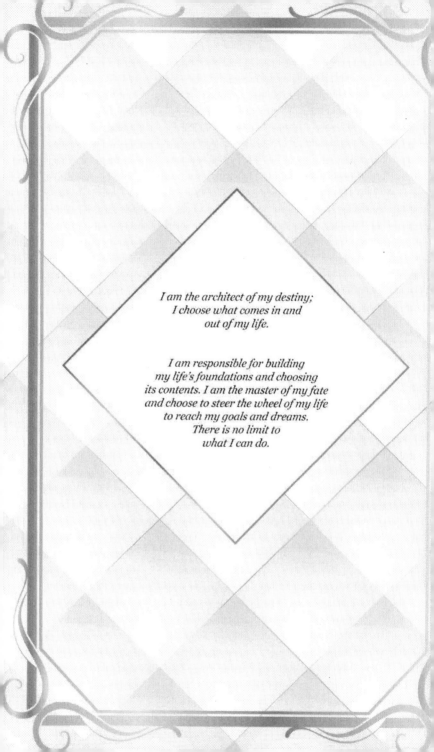

I am the architect of my destiny;
I choose what comes in and
out of my life.

I am responsible for building
my life's foundations and choosing
its contents. I am the master of my fate
and choose to steer the wheel of my life
to reach my goals and dreams.
There is no limit to
what I can do.

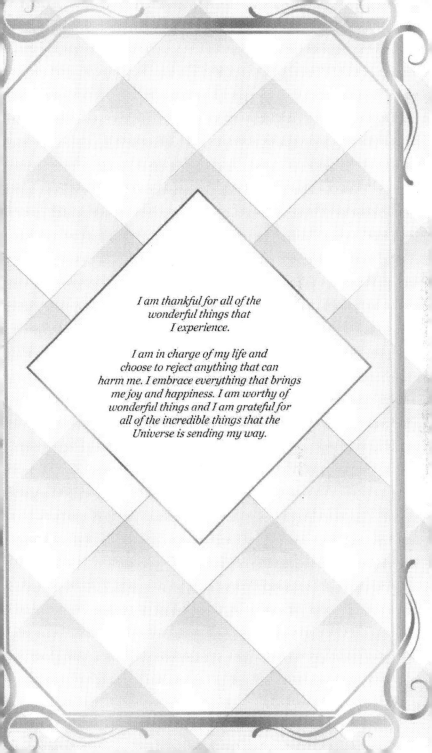

*I am thankful for all of the
wonderful things that
I experience.*

*I am in charge of my life and
choose to reject anything that can
harm me. I embrace everything that brings
me joy and happiness. I am worthy of
wonderful things and I am grateful for
all of the incredible things that the
Universe is sending my way.*

I wake up each day eager to embrace the amazing opportunities that will arise.

Today will be a great day. I have all that it takes to seize every opportunity in order to steer my life to achieve my goals and manifest the life of my dreams. I feel great, happy, and at peace with myself.

*I believe in myself and have
conviction in all that I do.*

*I deserve everything that I want
and feel confident to speak up for myself.
My gifts are one of a kind and my
uniqueness is of immense
value to the world.*

*I am in the process of becoming
the best version of myself.*

*I am smart, special, and unique.
I will face everything that comes my way with
a positive attitude. I attract what I want
and mirror my desires. I am what
I respect and admire.*

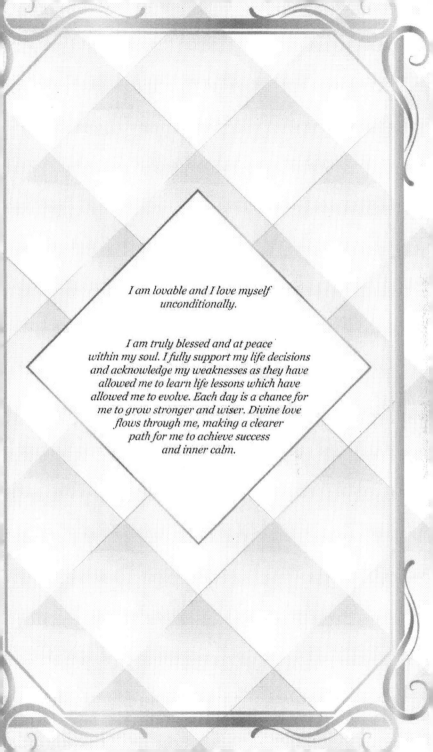

I am lovable and I love myself unconditionally.

I am truly blessed and at peace within my soul. I fully support my life decisions and acknowledge my weaknesses as they have allowed me to learn life lessons which have allowed me to evolve. Each day is a chance for me to grow stronger and wiser. Divine love flows through me, making a clearer path for me to achieve success and inner calm.

*I am enough and exactly who
I should be; even with imperfections,
I am perfect.*

*My worth is not based on my achievements.
I accept and love myself for who
I am because I am enough and that gives
me the courage to be authentic,
vulnerable, and imperfect –
and that is okay.*

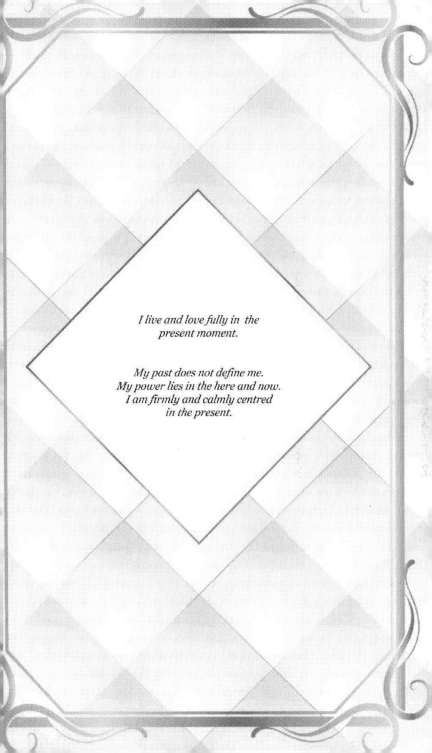

*I live and love fully in the
present moment.*

*My past does not define me.
My power lies in the here and now.
I am firmly and calmly centred
in the present.*

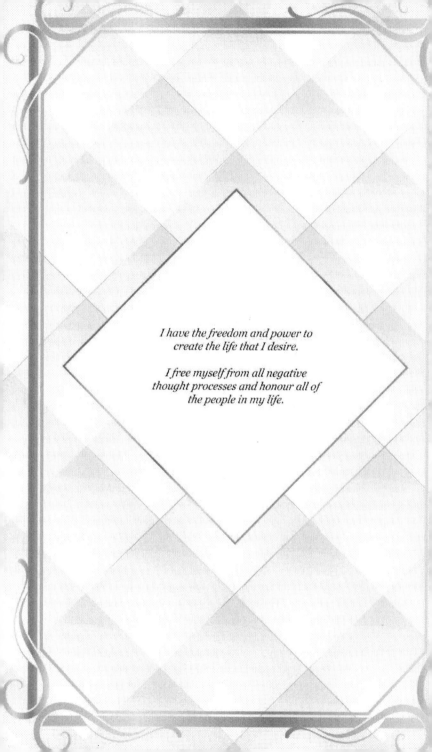

I have the freedom and power to create the life that I desire.

I free myself from all negative thought processes and honour all of the people in my life.

*I radiate confidence, grandeur,
and beauty.*

*I feel comfortable in my skin, and
that helps me exude confidence. When
I stand in front of a mirror, I see
a beautiful person staring
right back at me.*

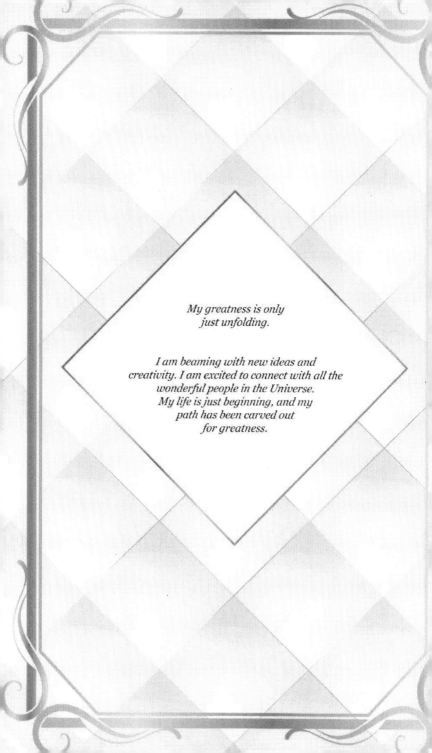

*My greatness is only
just unfolding.*

*I am beaming with new ideas and
creativity. I am excited to connect with all the
wonderful people in the Universe.
My life is just beginning, and my
path has been carved out
for greatness.*

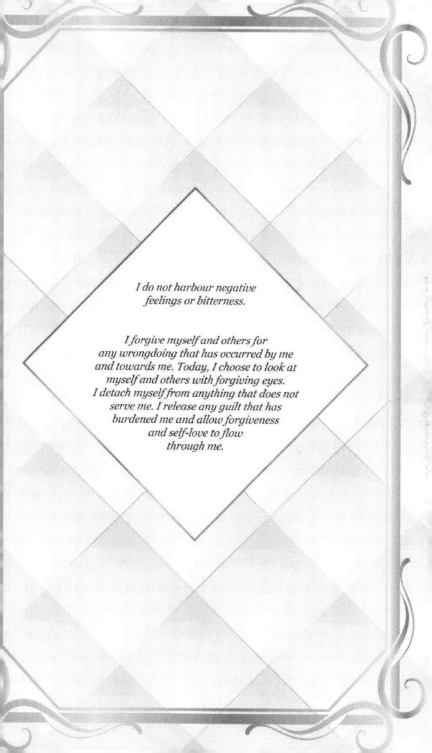

*I do not harbour negative
feelings or bitterness.*

*I forgive myself and others for
any wrongdoing that has occurred by me
and towards me. Today, I choose to look at
myself and others with forgiving eyes.
I detach myself from anything that does not
serve me. I release any guilt that has
burdened me and allow forgiveness
and self-love to flow
through me.*

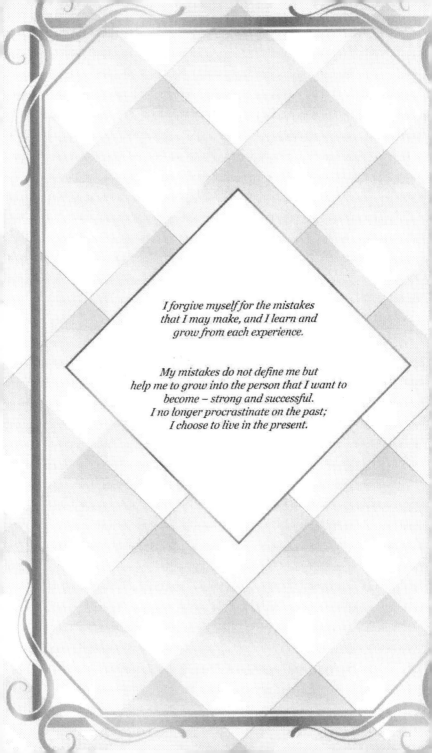

*I forgive myself for the mistakes
that I may make, and I learn and
grow from each experience.*

*My mistakes do not define me but
help me to grow into the person that I want to
become – strong and successful.
I no longer procrastinate on the past;
I choose to live in the present.*

*I love and accept my body and
work at keeping it healthy and strong.*

*I am complete and perfect, just the
way that I am. I feed and nourish my body
with healthy food and exercise
because it deserves love and tender care.
I listen to what my body needs and
trust my inner judgment.*

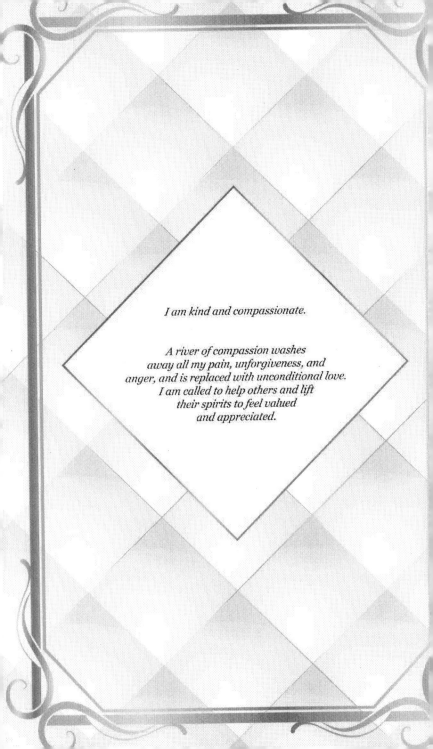

I am kind and compassionate.

A river of compassion washes
away all my pain, unforgiveness, and
anger, and is replaced with unconditional love.
I am called to help others and lift
their spirits to feel valued
and appreciated.

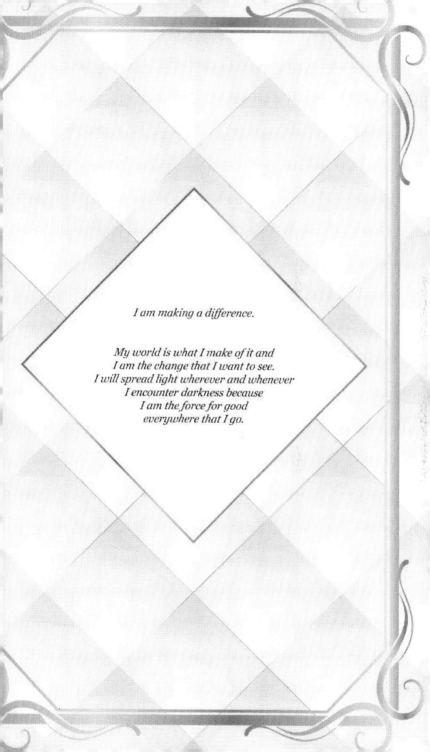

I am making a difference.

My world is what I make of it and
I am the change that I want to see.
I will spread light wherever and whenever
I encounter darkness because
I am the force for good
everywhere that I go.

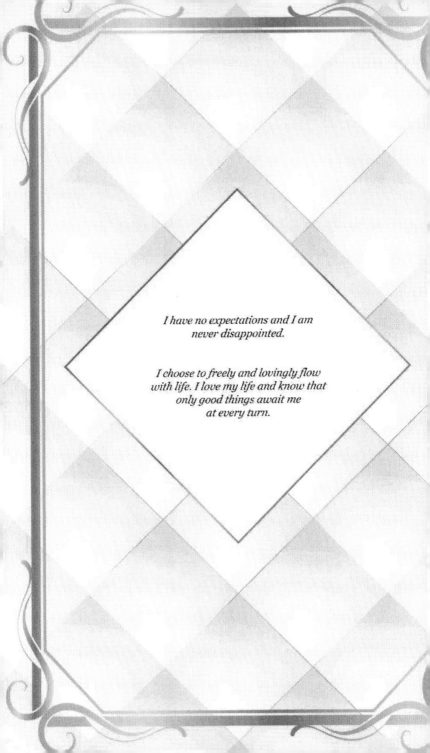

*I have no expectations and I am
never disappointed.*

*I choose to freely and lovingly flow
with life. I love my life and know that
only good things await me
at every turn.*

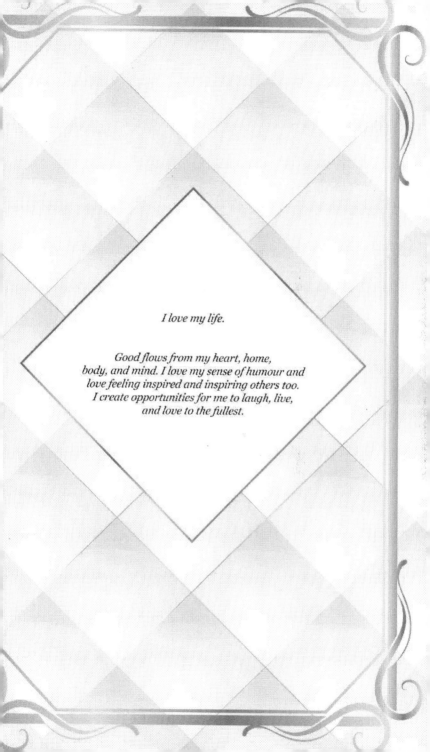

I love my life.

*Good flows from my heart, home,
body, and mind. I love my sense of humour and
love feeling inspired and inspiring others too.
I create opportunities for me to laugh, live,
and love to the fullest.*

Chapter 6 - Specific affirmations for health & happiness

If you are healthy and well, do not forget to thank the Universe for this.

If you are sick, try to keep an open mind and remember that when it comes to your health, there is always a possibility that no matter how sick you are, your body can heal. Never give up, remember that miracles can and do happen!

This chapter holds several affirmations that can help you to remain well or can help you to welcome health and happiness back into your life.

Examples of health affirmations include;

- ❖ I am full of health.
- ❖ I am getting better each day from my illness.
- ❖ I shall not be tied down by my mind, muscles, and veins.

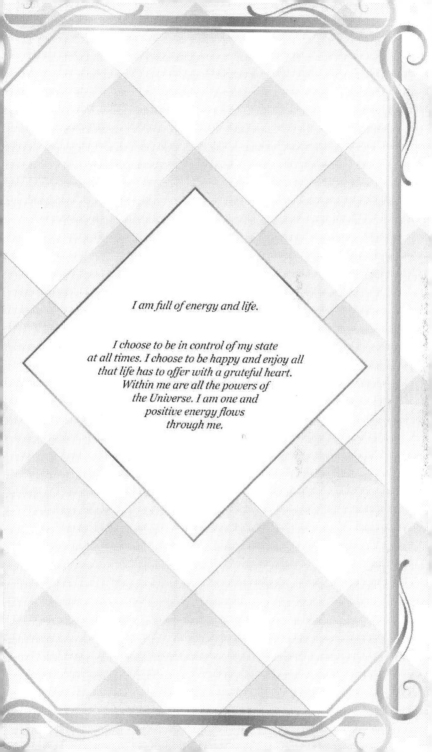

I am full of energy and life.

*I choose to be in control of my state
at all times. I choose to be happy and enjoy all
that life has to offer with a grateful heart.
Within me are all the powers of
the Universe. I am one and
positive energy flows
through me.*

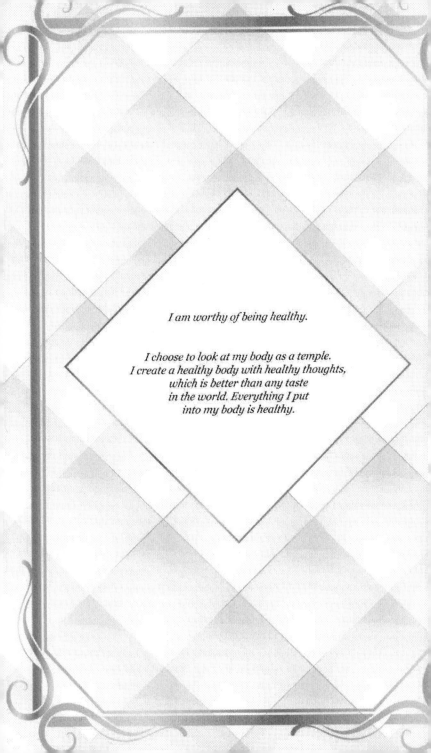

I am worthy of being healthy.

I choose to look at my body as a temple.
I create a healthy body with healthy thoughts,
which is better than any taste
in the world. Everything I put
into my body is healthy.

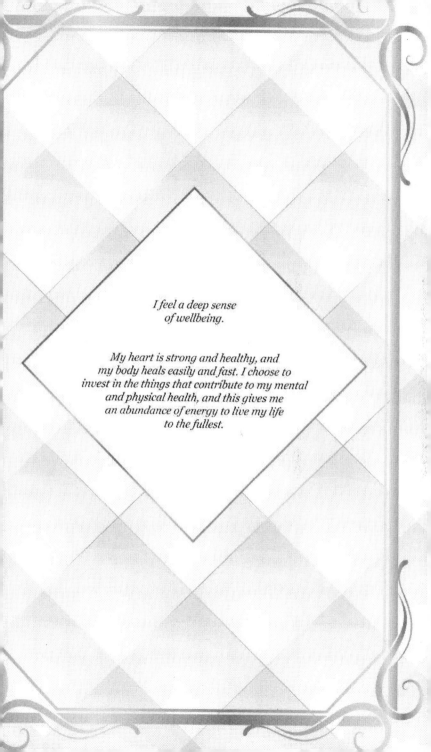

*I feel a deep sense
of wellbeing.*

*My heart is strong and healthy, and
my body heals easily and fast. I choose to
invest in the things that contribute to my mental
and physical health, and this gives me
an abundance of energy to live my life
to the fullest.*

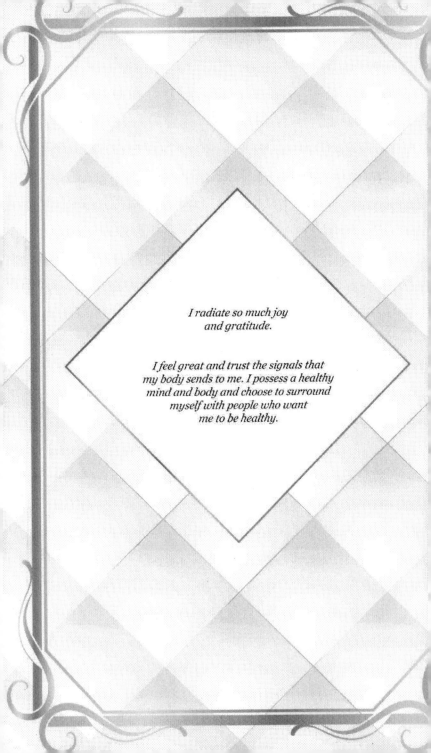

*I radiate so much joy
and gratitude.*

*I feel great and trust the signals that
my body sends to me. I possess a healthy
mind and body and choose to surround
myself with people who want
me to be healthy.*

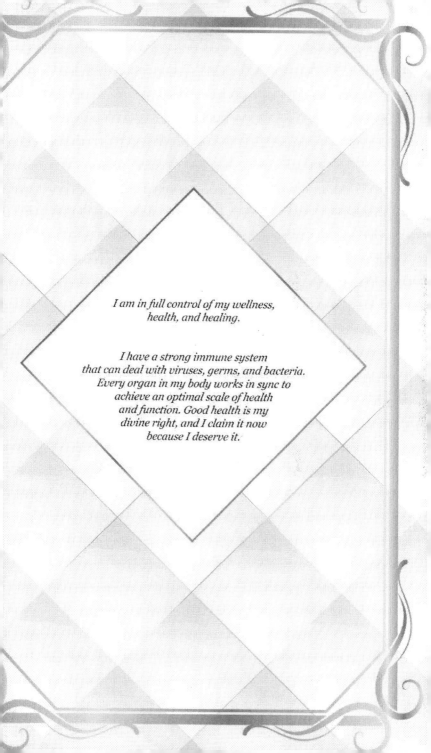

*I am in full control of my wellness,
health, and healing.*

*I have a strong immune system
that can deal with viruses, germs, and bacteria.
Every organ in my body works in sync to
achieve an optimal scale of health
and function. Good health is my
divine right, and I claim it now
because I deserve it.*

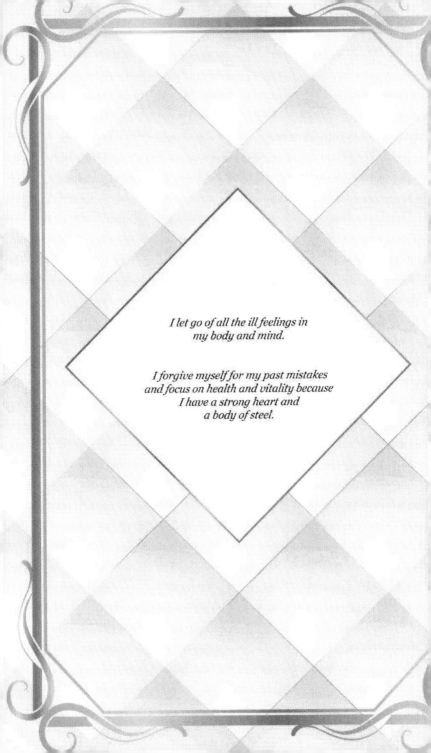

*I let go of all the ill feelings in
my body and mind.*

*I forgive myself for my past mistakes
and focus on health and vitality because
I have a strong heart and
a body of steel.*

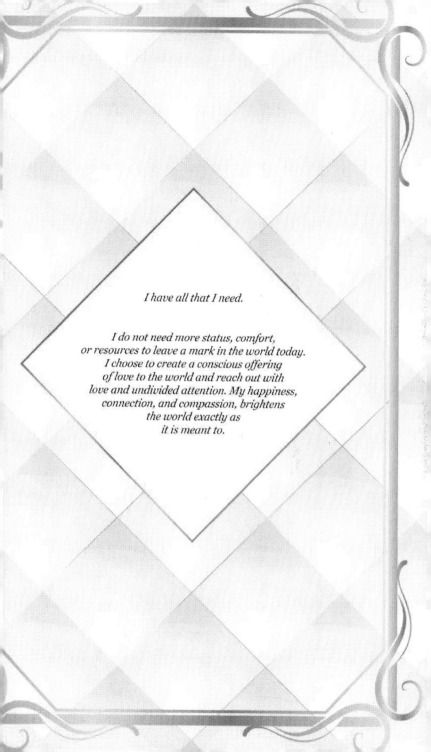

I have all that I need.

*I do not need more status, comfort,
or resources to leave a mark in the world today.
I choose to create a conscious offering
of love to the world and reach out with
love and undivided attention. My happiness,
connection, and compassion, brightens
the world exactly as
it is meant to.*

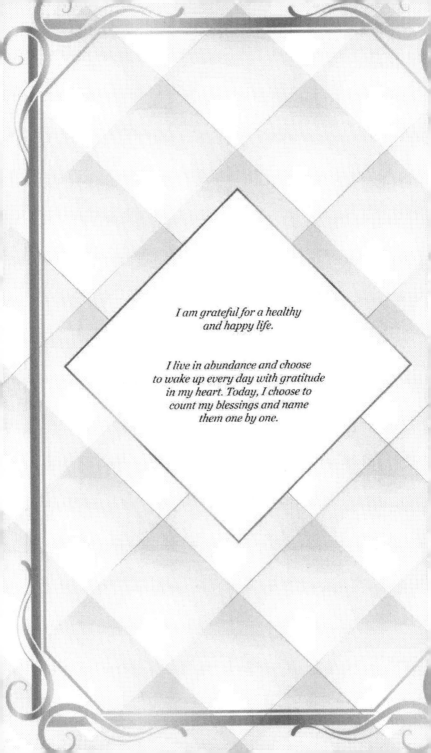

*I am grateful for a healthy
and happy life.*

*I live in abundance and choose
to wake up every day with gratitude
in my heart. Today, I choose to
count my blessings and name
them one by one.*

My health is my wealth.

*Every breath that I take energises me,
and my sight gets better with each
passing day. I am getting healthier and
wealthier every day in every healthy
choice I make and
how I live.*

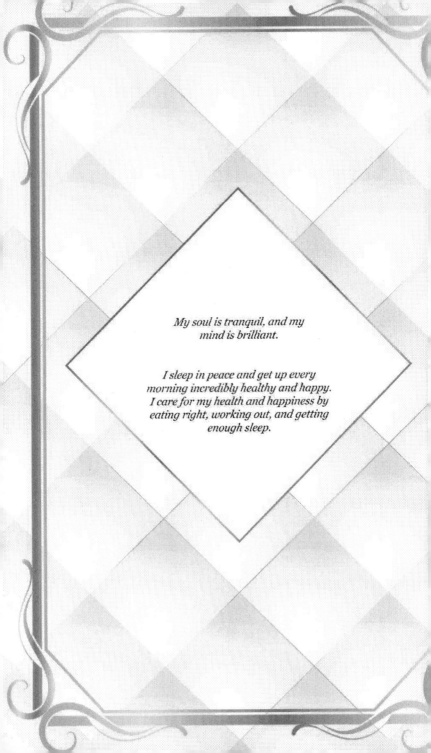

My soul is tranquil, and my mind is brilliant.

I sleep in peace and get up every morning incredibly healthy and happy. I care for my health and happiness by eating right, working out, and getting enough sleep.

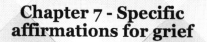

Chapter 7 - Specific affirmations for grief

I allow myself to feel this fully .

The pain and loss
I am experiencing is real and valid
and is a true testament to the love that
I shared and for that I am thankful.
Eventually I will smile again as
I know I can get through this.

I'm not going to hold back.

*When I am ready to talk, I know there
will be a ready soul to listen.*

Nothing makes sense right now,
and it does not have to.

I will take time to process
what is happening and will then
emerge a stronger, more
compassionate person.

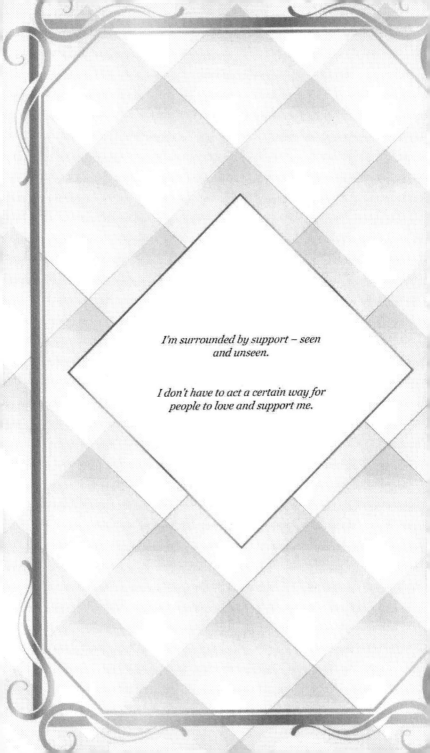

I'm surrounded by support – seen and unseen.

I don't have to act a certain way for people to love and support me.

Healing takes place slowly.

*I will encounter similar wounds
many times, but I choose a new
perspective each time. My process is
my own, and it is beautiful.*

I will never be the same person again,
and that is okay.

I know I can hold on to the love and let
go of the grief.

*The Universe lifts, supports,
and guides me.*

Today, I choose to heal.

I am gentle with myself as I heal.

I can pay tribute to living my life beautifully.

I choose to focus my attention on my goals, memories, and blessings.

Chapter 8 - Specific affirmations for anxiety

*I choose to free myself from
all forms of destructive fear and doubt
by rising above these frightening
thoughts.*

*I create peace in my mind, heart,
and soul.*

I am fierce, bold, and unafraid.

I am in charge of my thoughts and will not let them control me. Whatever I am going through is not new, and I know my strength will help me survive and change my world.

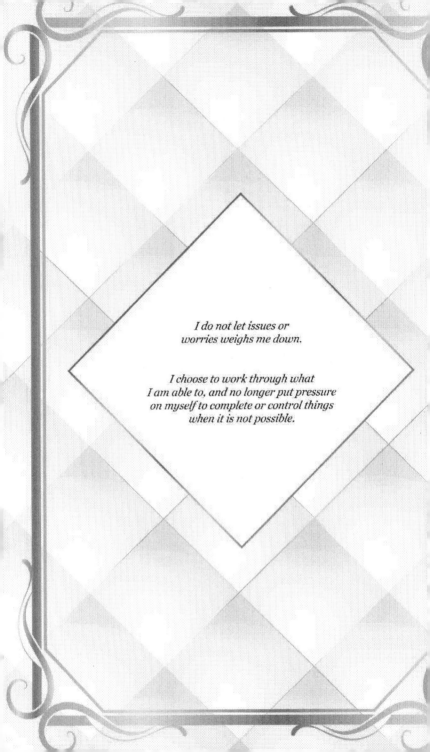

*I do not let issues or
worries weighs me down.*

*I choose to work through what
I am able to, and no longer put pressure
on myself to complete or control things
when it is not possible.*

*I let go of past mistakes and hurt,
and look forward to the good things that
lay in wait for me.*

*With every breath, I choose to
take in strength and release fear and
anxiety. I am learning that it is okay and
safe for me to heal and grow.*

Everything is unravelling itself
as it should.

No matter what I have been through,
there are no mistakes but only lessons
learned. I did the best I could and now
choose to fill my mind with positive,
healing, and nurturing thoughts.

My challenges are my opportunities.

*I am becoming stronger and wiser
because of what I have been through.
Every situation and circumstance in my
life is a stepping stone to greater
opportunities for success.*

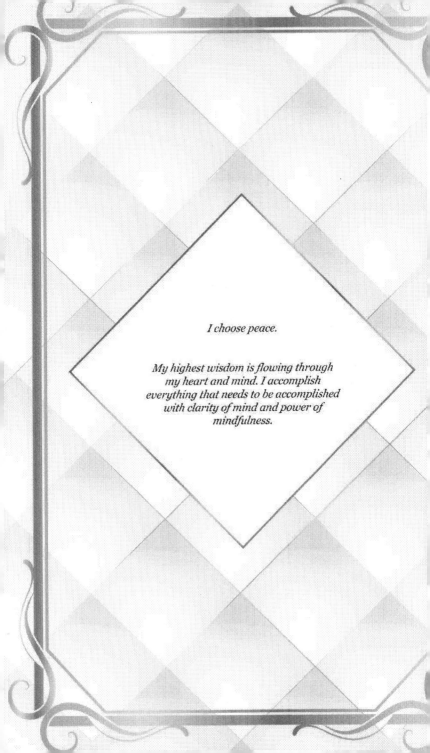

I choose peace.

My highest wisdom is flowing through my heart and mind. I accomplish everything that needs to be accomplished with clarity of mind and power of mindfulness.

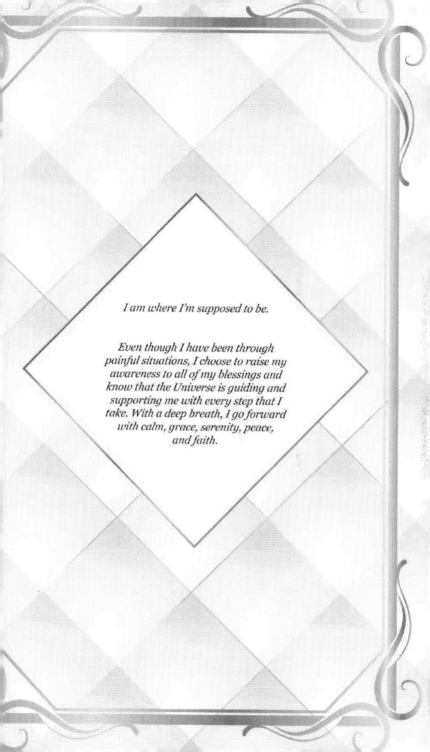

I am where I'm supposed to be.

Even though I have been through painful situations, I choose to raise my awareness to all of my blessings and know that the Universe is guiding and supporting me with every step that I take. With a deep breath, I go forward with calm, grace, serenity, peace, and faith.

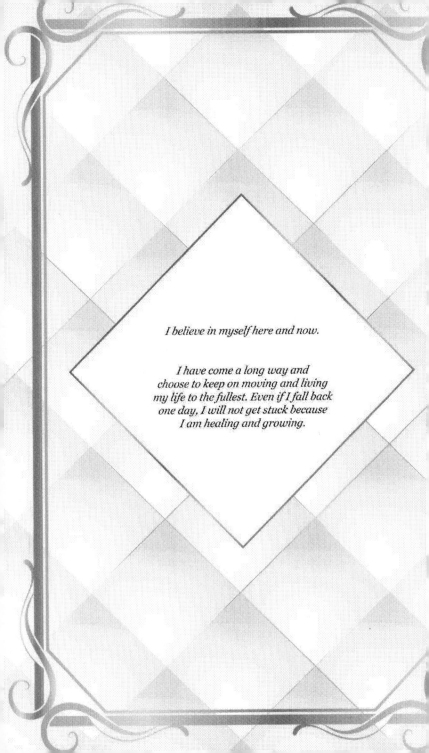

I believe in myself here and now.

*I have come a long way and
choose to keep on moving and living
my life to the fullest. Even if I fall back
one day, I will not get stuck because
I am healing and growing.*

I love myself and deserve to be happy and healthy.

I am in charge of my life story, and I decide how it is told. This is not the end of my story because there is more to life that the Universe has in store for me.

Chapter 9 - How to modify your affirmations

"It's the repetition of affirmations that leads to belief. And once that belief becomes a deep conviction, things begin to happen."

– Muhammad Ali

Affirmations must be structured correctly in order for you to attract precisely what you want to manifest in your life. They are an effective tool for becoming the person that you need to be, in order to achieve your goals and purpose in your life.

If you are repeating your affirmations but getting none of your desired outcomes, you need to modify and alter your affirmations. Rather than saying things like, "I am a millionaire. I have achieved all my goals this month," and expect it to come true, you need to modify it to suit what you are doing. You could say, "I am working hard to achieve all of my goals this month and am working towards earning my first million".

Being unrealistic or dishonest with yourself is the very reason your affirmations are not working. This means that when you recite your affirmations, they are not rooted in the truth, and your subconscious mind resists them.

The truth is, constantly lying to yourself will never be your optimal strategy to success. The truth will always hold so you need to make the relevant alterations.

Another reason that you may need to modify your affirmations is because you may have been using passive language – and that does not yield results. You are just saying them to feel good but, in the end, create empty promises, for instance "I am a money magnet and it flows to me effortlessly"- this could not be manifested if you are sitting around doing nothing to work towards achieving this. Your actions must align with your desired outcome, and your affirmations must affirm and articulate both the action and outcome.

Focus on the results you are committed to and why

Here, you are not starting with what you want, because all of us want things and don't always get what we want. However, we get the things we are committed to. Do you want to be a millionaire? You must start by clarifying your goals and executing all the necessary actions to get you the desired results. Do you want to be a kinder person? Then you must work on actions that create calm and help you to become a kinder and more compassionate being.

The trick is to write down all the specific outcomes that you want in your life. The outcomes must be those things that challenge you and would greatly boost your life. They are the things you are ready to commit to manifesting in your life, even when you are not sure how to do it. Once you commit, the next step is to reinforce them by including a WHY you want this to happen to you.

What are the necessary actions you are committed to taking, and when do you intend to take them?

Trust me; it is pointless to have an affirmation of what you want without affirming what you are committed to doing. You cannot trick your subconscious into thinking that the outcomes you want to manifest will happen automatically with zero effort!

The best way to modify your affirmations is to ask yourself the above question. Once you clarify your specific actions, habits, and activities required to steer you to achieve your goals, you need to set a timeline for executing all the necessary actions.

The more specific your actions are, the better. Your affirmations must include frequency, quantity, and time frame.

Recite them every morning with emotion

You must bear in mind that the affirmations you say in the morning are not just there to make you feel good. They are strategically created to reprogram your subconscious mind with beliefs and an overall mind-set that you must achieve your desired outcomes. They are meant to direct your conscious mind to stay focused on what matters most and engage actions that will steer you in the direction of your goals.

For your affirmations to be effective, you must tap into your emotions while reciting them. If you keep reciting them repeatedly without mindfully attaching emotion and feelings of truth, it makes it pointless. You must be willing to generate authentic excitement and determination and infuse powerful emotions into every affirmation you recite.

Start by scheduling a set time to recite your affirmations – whether when meditating, working out, taking a shower, or making breakfast. The point is to program your subconscious which will help to focus the conscious mind on what matters the most to you and what you are committed to. This will allow you to manifest what you want, wish, and desire into your reality. The only time you see results is when they become part of your daily routine.

Constantly update and evolve your affirmations.

As you keep evolving, so should your affirmations. Each time you have a new goal, dream, or desire that you want to create in your life, add in an affirmation.

Take a look at each area of your life – health, parenting, relationships, and finances. Do you have affirmations for each one of these areas? You must constantly update your affirmations to improve your mind-set. Each time you come across an inspiring philosophy or quote and think that it is a great improvement, add it to your affirmations.

Conclusion

There you have it, guys – positive affirmations to help you to effect the change that you want to see in your life. These affirmations will help you to challenge and overcome self-sabotaging behaviours and negative thoughts. Most of us have negative thoughts and have allowed them to talk us into believing that we are not good enough to manifest the life we want. These negative thoughts run so deep into your thought process that it strips you of confidence and self-belief. Interestingly, most of us don't realise that we have turned these negative thoughts into self-fulfilling prophecies. In other words, we have allowed our thoughts to drag us down.

If we turn these negative thoughts into positive ones, the effect is so powerful that you start manifesting everything that you want and desire. The trick is to repeat them as much as you can and incorporate them into your daily routine. Believe in them and start making positive changes in every area of your life.

While some people might consider them as 'wishful thinking', they most definitely are not. Just as physical workouts reprogram your muscle memory, affirmations can be seen as an exercise of the brain as they have the ability to reprogram your thinking so that, with time, you start thinking and acting differently.

Everything that you want, wish, and desire in life lies in the thoughts that you have. You are your thoughts. Take inventory of them today and align them with your wants and desires. Only then will you manifest your dreams into reality! What are you waiting for?

Thank You

Thank you so much for taking the time to read my book.

I hope that this book will help you to achieve all that you want, wish and desire into your life.

If you have enjoyed the book, please leave a review on Amazon. Your reviews are greatly appreciated.

Thank you for your time, and I look forward to you reading some of my other publications.

N.D. LONDON

Check Out My Other Books

Please visit **www.ndlondon.co.uk** to join my mailing list and to check out my other books .

Anxious about being anxious: Simple techniques to calm the mind.

Someone I love has cancer: What now? Coping when a loved one has a cancer diagnosis and never giving up hope. Fighting to live. Therapies, advice, stories of survivorship & empowerment.

Printed in Great Britain
by Amazon

55452961R00052